TOAD'S SANCTUARY

I0079493

TOAD'S SANCTUARY

TAMAS PANITZ

ORNITHOPTER PRESS   PRINCETON

First Edition

Published by Ornithopter Press

www.ornithopterpress.com

ISBN 978-1-942723-08-0

Library of Congress Control Number: 2021931173

Design and composition by Mark Harris

CONTENTS

I. Toad's Sanctuary

TAMAS PANITZ RIDES AGAIN

In a small town with a long street
they'll miss me when I arrive.

Water will never forget my face
now that I've clear-cut the radio signals.

What goes around goes around. There
anchored in a coiled cove

of turns of thought, my thought takes turns
burning at the help-desk time immemorial,

radiant with descriptors (almost wrote
diamantenpracht).

I bring my crystal to a spitting match
strong as an arc from drinking semen.

I remind myself that optimism leads to
terrorism, and I do not wish to ride for the

Pony Express, nor do I wish to prepare earthmen
for the advent of Vulthoom. Verbs pour

through the cracks in these empanadas
and vice versa, like the game-plan for the theogony

written, kakodromenon! on the mirror of our lake.
We'll paddle-board through embattled stars

hoofbeats returning to their shetland ponies.
Paved with scandal is the way to silence.

They call me Floresco and then they call me.
I'm a dream you 'can't' have.

HERALDIC BLAZON FOR THE RIVER ESOPUS

Pull thy vanity open
in the Golden Dawn
      with those spooky heroes in the mere idea
      of spookiness, getting
            spooked, and maybe more—
lovers of nerves and danger
      letting their auricles
dangle in our attitudes, promising
everything, and only that
               over and over again.

MAGIC SWORD THAT APPEARS ONLY TO BELIEVERS

The course of the Sawkill is *withheld.* A map, that is not & yet is
the thing, a mantic device or symbol of the thing thinking, *that*
they would suppress. Ferns and the ghosts of canoes. Gravel and the
civilizing air of construction. Ancient naive palaces and the presence
of the sorcerer who vanished at death: the presences that never die,
but await solicitation. The solitudes of a map. The lingam, lost but
not lost; the ligament that lingers.

THREE TAROT CARDS

1.
IN THE MIRROR OF THE NEW MOON (LA LUNE)

The window cracked open to hear
to hear through the moon's
aperture
of mixed identifications. Closing
up way me and you once were.
To lose sight in the mind
is to be out of sight.
Waiting in the lab for specimens.
For the visitor outside the door
in the slow disappearance of outside.
So the flaming green tail that
once rounded corners sits
in the wooden chair of its teeth.
The tongue surprises me again
in the prism of the sentence.
Gentle as a red fish.
Easy to be entreated
by the blue pools by which the dogs fight.
Swimming in the pool
of one word and then another
in an inverse cone
waiting for you in the dark in bed
nodding nodding in the city.
In the city for the star
spangled shadows of my
stars and starvations
what there was to call together
the obedience of the dog-days
the obedience of dogs &
ease of acquiescence scatters.

Cherish the blurry photographs
of friends that turn to water
in the light of no moon.
Hear the dogs yelp
amid the feasting of rays.

2.
LA FORZA

La Forza, the Lion, is contagious.
It must have been my grandmother
helped open her hands with his jaws
reach into my heart, he said
ladders of fire, snakes of stone,
everything is a stand-in,
symbolic degrees of what isn't.
His sisters rejoiced
as they ran up the stairs.
There's so much
in the air it's easy to balance,
in the form of lions come to help me
among new species of desire.
In the aloofness of Mary's
body the envelopes of the eye flap
flap rows and rows of doors that once
stirred children into frenzy
vanish from a certain standpoint
blue and yellow and green
the hidden ratios
less interesting than their patience
on the brink of unrecoverability.
By straining all our muscles
together, by training ourselves
by interest in the abyss,
some observational sliver
raises itself beyond reabsorption.
In the expectant shadow,
The Dictionary opens all at once.

3.
NIGHT WALKERS

Anyone could be driving by.
There's a silky rumble even to the big
engines of the weather.
There's an animal familiarity
within the experiment's controls.
Breaths and observations
ingress upon the band of quartz
that guards Old Greene County
unspoken in the foyers of Tanner's Bank.
If there's an aesthetic speech
then there is giant consciousness
within it. If there is exercise
of unaccountable behaviors
and footprints on the moors,
who possesses their least inanities?
Even the birds have managed
a surprise for me this morning
caressed by the roof of your mouth:
clothes, climbers, clits!
Laden with sheep and Mexican selenite
to hit a moving target
one must be in motion surely.
Hunting sand between my teeth tonight
stirs there from one house to the next
the salubrious coverlet
of barking dogs and burnt leaves.

Your Tarot Current for the 17th-19th Centuries

Yard backed up to the thruway, then others will follow.
The bent & personal backs of things. Free memories.
Families. Flambé, the sunset touches w/ actual flame.

TOAD'S RIPOSTE, *for Kit Schluter*

1.
Canoes of poltroons
in winter dark.
Soon

a callous chalice
parts both ways
the lips the lips
of things lap
one another.

Is that you
pal, bother.

Plenteous
malodious.
Yes. No,
yes this is you.

A voice
a face
a venerable bright

Taste of Uzbek
—oh did you really?

Canoes on the lake.
So round the lake.
So dark the pals.

SORT OF SESTINA

Her arranged fruit turns sailors bald; whispers
speak for deformed ears
something to turn me blue.
I met the devil in snakes and ladders,
the fifth road that sits inside the cross
lovers lane and rolling dice to get hot.

Hot for hexagon the room flares each side
whispers in parseltongue hidden in French.
Cross me and live, said he.
Ears of white ships in the fog of your voice.
Ladders unseen were come to suspend without end
blue wastes peopled by rotund princes.

Blue lobsters will stand by their assertions
after death
ladders walk sentimental under us
whispers the beach to the trees it's broken.
Ears of despair, ears of no good fortune
cross the small vowel that fragments our life.

Cross me off your uninvited list, dear
blue azaleas wreathe my Dodge Caravan
ears all in a row pass gradually
hot behind the lower ears they include
whispers of parts a body from the deep
ladders clasp in a growing extravagance.

Ladders of insults, friends' forgotten kids
cross in desperation the public parks
whispers like scissors pass down through our pants,
Blue blue Christmas
hot snow and shallow bites of your friends—
ears forfend these evil tenants' tidings.

Ears on fire with a stranger's secrets
ladders could not violate nor sever
hot from the grill only my tongue can reach
cross if you must this tiresome nebula
blue candy broken before you bought it
whispers could claim their king from the blue pile

cross upon cross a city of cheap rooms
blue to keep the hags away
whispers, whispers, form dangerous clusters.

II. Idyls & Other Pastoralia

IDYL, *after Moschus*

The biased oiled sun drips
in the bull whose horns curve
into a silver crescent and a silver ball
hovers between them:
in the heart of the heart an oil drips
silver, upward, between the dishes of the shoulders.
At the point of everything
turning crystal, the lube for a crystal
piston sprints across the hardened sea.
Europa sticks to the bull's back—
          her clam is stronger—
burns in the crystal dish of the bull's
aching arched in the slope of a wing
      a single broad flame
bent into the wind.

IDYLS

(Note:

Speech (dialogic)   from Stasis.

I had to ask: *why can't I start the poem?*
And to ask the question
is a question of emphasis on the I:

onus, impedimenta.

15

1.

The Ascension of Henry Hudson

She asked me if I was familiar with Dutchman's Landing.
I said: of course, it is flat, and the Buck Moon is crisp and pale
and where its lashes have fled to the other end of the world, the pale
light lifts the landing like a mirror to the hill where I live.
She asked: Do you know who I am?
And I replied: I have seen your turquoise rings and obscene bonnet
and your refusal to match.
She said, as she vanished and did not vanish: my refusal is deeper
than it seems.
My boat was gone, and my crew turned to drunken imps among the
hollows, grew goiters, and sold hotdogs.
Now listen, lady! I screamed, but I was already halfway dissolved into
a local signal, and I was only the weak chirp of the Beach Boys in a
passing black car.

2.

She said, this is the path that crosses the Hop o' Nose, the bright
garden of ignoring scripture.
I placed a large pinch of tobacco along the lifeline of my palm and
watched it slide through to the other side.
Here, she said, the steamboats stop and reverse their engines in the
shallow water.
I spoke: Lady, will you make me invincible in battle?
I will help you, she said, and put one large diamond into a clay vessel
filled with water.
I wept as I swallowed the water, and the diamond, and then I ate the
vessel.
The skunks were circling me.
Her hand performed the rite of an iridescent moth above my
forehead.
Then, where the moth had been, I could see Olana across the river,
burning,
and we laughed together as mother and son.

3. *(Beginning with a line from Lila Dunlap)*

I took that bitch down to the batture.
My pockets were bottomless and I gave her porcupines, rollerskates,
cars, and good times. At last I was down to candy, and she signaled
through her french ruffles *c'est assez.*

She asked: is it affective or *e*ffective,
I can never remember.

On the marble streets I slid beneath the Live Oaks to remand my
memory with a flowering whip of moss that I named *Vincent.*

The dream of Athens was upon Baltimore that summer as Poe
visited New Orleans.

She said, *Monsieur Poe...*

But I had drifted nearly to the lakeshore on a thin strip of green
marble, cosmopolitan, decent, and the water was over my ears.

4.

In the cool of the morning a tower of mist collapsed around us.
The stones plunged down and she said: Build on wheels.
Whales breeched through the white mask that swung across the
harbor.
Her silence was as aggravating as her speech.
My car wouldn't start.
She said: Love is variance in love's absence.
I let out a long inaudible yell.
They know what they call me, I said at the restaurant.
I limped along the shore, a flutter of owl feathers, now that the rain
was obscured by clouds.

5.

The leaves rolled by on the trees and the trees rolled by on the
nameless hill.
Where are you taking me, I asked.
The fish sparkled in the echo of waves, rode the waves and their
wonders.
An olive tree, where no one lives, will burst into song, leaves flashing
fish.
If you were a ghost, she said, you could see the luminous fluids of the
skunks, as they dance like dust through the abandoned houses.
I asked: is this a funeral?
My speeches were a matter of Eros, gathering in what I could.
She whispered through a piece of dust: it smells like Juniper. Statues.
Nightingales. The wonderful month of May.
Her breath spun a small golden wheel from the stillness of my
ceiling.

6.

I asked her: Does the plane of Jefferson Heights extend forever?

Beneath its elevated surface the leaves of the town distract themselves with further bifurcations.

Look up! She cried.

Beyond the dentist's office, the Italianate manor grows rings and rings of porches.

The cars outside are merely radios to a man in bed, I said.

The train tracks cool and blue before resurrection.

7.

She slid easily out from my mind.
Do you know the landmarks here? she asked.
My hands slipped through each other, as they grappled in convergent
streams: I knew I possessed another's secret body.

The white crests and the gallant green of the waves split into two
streams and stalked back up Olympus.
Hard to remember which one comes first, she said.

I counted the trees until I got lost.

She hung singing chips of glass across my chest, and told me what
her mistress looked like bathing here to spoil my memory.
A liquid gem that pulsed through the air.
I have no memory for minerals, I said.
Her outlines faded into the pulse in which I suspected myself of
ulterior motives.

I was Fats Waller again and I started to swim down the Hudson.

8.

Was Francis a Sagittarius. No, but
the backwards leaps of crawfish amid the reply (which was a dazzling
Sardanas) were a kind of refreshment.
The Llevantina played her song, while the hams of nocturnal dancers
                              clapped in the crown of the hillside
diurnal apocalyptic clavés.

She said: no one's missing anything.
My glasses were on my face after all.
I leapt backwards through a lineage that was pleased to display itself
in the stone path and fallen branches piled to the side.

I felt like Zeus, or Ceviche, as I went.

The path, overgrown, bent around the hill and lost itself in the
woods.

9. *(Beginning with a line by Blake)*

"Hiding the Demon red with clouds ..."

Dribbling with red honey, the birds
splashed slowly in the golden pools.
  Description is an excuse for Enchantment.

Hiding the demon
  rather than move on,
the red clouds changed:
  these I x'd out on my interior copy.
She suggested, gruffly: there might be a tide that obliterates the coils
of the Ram's Horn creek. There might be a time when I would drift,
scraps of red, in turgescent marshy heaps.

    (2.)

I would wear purple scraps of cloth
by the peeling leather
  brownstone graves, the sort I would love
to the orgy of ghouls
    presented by leafless Black-eyed Susans.
It's so nice to reduce.
To work it good, down to precious fatty glimmer
  of white dew without purpose.

Magic is the same thing as fun, she said.
Hang on to this definition for protection.

PREDICTIONARY

Apocalypse

A ghost-inviting cream
those interesting people
glow from my skeleton's walls
like some luminist paint-job
of dancing caryatids
that turn out to be clouds.

Candelabra

abracadabra
the random assortment
is beautiful, only apparently
useless, only apparently random.

Surprise

I made someone angry
sits the banishment
down of its own
rearranged people
amid the accord.

Avatar

what word what person
comes into the light
of pronouncement
pouring in from the cave-
mouth, a being of light
an ode to every word.

Cabbage

that became a man
the poles in its teeth
pulled itself up by the hair.

Anchor

lurching forward
and staying still
festina lente, insider
trading, Paradiso
the porch swing
swinging.

Element

species of thirst
uncaught offshore.

Flibbertigibbet

blazer burnt
at the edges, red eyes
from behind the eyes from behind
the mirror talk unceasingly
help to dip my letters low.

Guillotine

for men
pick a new word
when the scree is too steep

to make chopped cheese
no more bandoleras
that followed all yesterday
became the Elf-King's steam.

Harp

every bird has a story
the nets remember
from my childhood
take precedence,
take prisoners, poison
the names of the living
that keep us from the dead.

Camphor

for my lord's Duck L'Orange
put it in my pocket
try not to look
whether or not they're enchanted
the frogs are finishing up.

Strain

slept through
stepped through
palace la place.

Slander

Where does the associative end
someone's been inside

alchemical fiends
the mind strikes midnight
& the illusion watches.

Jouissance

the stuff of legends
of average folk
swinging doors
doorbells, tightropes
the amazing rains of
Times Square, what will
excite connection
syntax enter and
the children of flame
the wails of Maldoror
hither and thither
sharks fly through the rain.

Gyres

an apostrophe
when the sentence never ends
but stores its tools and their usages
when the thickest crickets
superior cars
rounded with wisdom drive
through the turn of the seasons.

Quilt

the return of the steamboat
has been put on pause, sharks

venturous in absence
adore the vacuum
and good spelling will come
of its own accord
stay on your board
or you won't survive the waves
at Nazare.

Violet

an embarrassment encasement
by grapeleaves or squashblossoms
the bars of the underworld
vibrate in my cathexis
a bundle of gleeful staves
gathered from every direction
they're still heading in
a black mass of humming bats
against color of sunset baseball field.

Cobra

there's no odd hours
it's an open house
not every rain
works the same
the abilities that come
the cablecars filled with pumpkins
too heavy to stop plunged
into the sacred pond
you can watch from the stoa
the eructation of nipples
eels they will be in spring.

Locutor

wounds without bodies.

Spasm

apropos nothing
abandon hope
Pan is coming, abandon
conservatisms
and seep through the stone
behind Jesus
the seal of the beloved
eructations from the cave
by which cows cool down
over in Schoharie County.

Scythe

fall color sharpens
the eye behind enemy lines
a harpoon and a Shar Pei
spirit devices
rhyming tickle adjacencies
the Bach that has no exit sign.

Evaluate

the rain now only
secondary rain
is my constant concern
no matter how you tie it
my friends can get out

the combination is in order
despite all efforts
and the risk
of doing it in public.

Saliva

coffee at midnight
in the sink
becoming cleaner
among the stains.

Avenue

push forward
with Satanic influence
& hatred of progress
Ben Franklin at last
Philadelphia must burn
riverine
vile enchantment: I wish
the Masons would just
turn off the Enlightenment
there's something awful in my hair
shining in Federalist shampoo
now, I'm not saying the bodies of
policemen are a window
to another dimension
or The Dictionary must be freed
there's no money in hunches
honey, I'm not losing business
I'm in the losing business
the dark & pointless, stuff auxiliary.

Revenue

Bonne nuit spirit of the stairs
into the dry plums stars come
coursing down good night
alphabet ladders
only fools miss the pleasure
of describing the impossible
they say it's too nice to microwave
but you're with me now
a black lab and a golden retriever
subtraction's unknown consequences.

Spoon

write in your sleep
buried tablets
pry up the ancient spoon
from depths of yoghurt
o rainbow arc'd Turners
let me say such mundane
words inconceivable
blaze in human middens
the pie without constraint.

Ignition

combustion is an element
part of the riddle
where the wind blows
to bribe the gatekeepers
no movement needed
to watch the stars

explode among us
shift definitions
drifters in search of water.

Definition

resurrect your dyslexia
the singed angels
dice endlessly
among the hinges
dangers, strongholds
the suggestion of disorder
is so beautiful as it
rolls along the quay
through the gaps and naps
before it sticks and fails.

III. Claims

THE FACE: a tribute to Achorai

When I recollect that the Messiah has come and gone, and History as theophany, as it is in the Jewish tradition, has ceased its roll, I sometimes feel like one of those fated Kabbalists who simply burnt up, burnt bright with too little interest in the objects of sustenance. Dates. Numbers. Narratives. Opinions. The faces shown us in the history of our day are as placid as the faces of demons seem to each other in their triumphal march across us. For us late-comers, history is at best the excuse to cause, to impose, a history, i.e., magic; at worst it is a determination with which we are burdened. I remain within any history as stupid as a lover in love, and thus remain unscathed in a way as I articulate from within. I have only myself to worry about.

Face is no business of mine. I am all face, all adoration for the unstructured occurrence "behind" me.

Behind the word is a committee that does not exist. Behind us in the sense of a cause is Truth, and Truth, which is only a vision, does not need to exist outside of our fidelity to it. We do not need to exist, and in Truth we together vanish. No one but evil needs to exist. Is fooled by its own need. And as it regards evil, Truth turns into judgment: so our existence is the work of evil, the slight edge of a blade not fully formed even, not fully here, but to the extent it is needed in Judgment's service, and to the extent evil needs itself. An athanor, where evil overcomes itself, and a blinding mirror.

A face and a face only for the destruction of that which needs it.

MANIFESTO: on the Aesthetics of Solomon's Temple

Cactus or candles, show me what my room is thinking, what it imagines itself to be. The gods with which I have surrounded myself speak. Chairs refuse to be displaced as they breathe. Things reveal their secret teleology: what I need does not need me. What I 'need' is what my room desires, and I live in its patience, terrible, heavy

The Temple desires to be rebuilt.

The walls of a city are called from the ground, from matter, where they sleep— Plato said so— they ἐγείρειν, awaken, stiffen up from pelvic ground. By some unheard trumpet stone is placed on stone: this stone I brought back from the beach, smooth and black, believing desire to be mine.

A hand moves to grasp, release, obey. Men formed of ego, task, pathos, pieces of light shoot across the field, and light is unable to braid itself back together. So much for sports.

The walls are still in the ground: in my living room, my clothes, books, thoughts, enemies, friends. Listen carefully. Raise them.

addendum: The Molten Sea

Beside the Temple is a ring of oxen, supporting a bronze basin on their backs. They lower their heads, each an o, *samech*, bent like water against its burden, its direction. Water is not oppressed by the sides of the container, but its own weight keeps it there, and the sky, another water, from which it flees, driven. Weight is a necessity that drives. The bend of a letter to its doom, and all the words it must be to get there.

The identity of the Moors in Spain cannot be separated from the Jewish identity that evolved during Moorish rule and influence.

Identity, "being the same as," requires an Other, Allah.

We are shown precisely the other becoming the same in the person of Joshua: he is Moses' successor, and responsible in the Hebrew Bible for the expulsion of the Moors from Canaan; meanwhile in the Qur'an he is exceptional among Israelites for being one of the faithful followers of Allah.

Curiously enough, The Noble Prophet Drew Ali chooses to establish the provenance of this somewhat-Islamic brotherhood with reference to the deeds of the Hebrew Bible's Joshua. "These are the Moabites, Hamithites, Canaanites, who were driven out of the land of Canaan, by Joshua, and received permission from the Pharaohs of Egypt to settle in that portion of Egypt. In later years they formed themselves kingdoms. These kingdoms are called this day Morocco, Algiers, Tunis, Tripoli, etc." Thus the Prophet Drew Ali shows us in a most subtle way that the two Joshuas might be regarded as a single complex identity.

The 36 Hidden Tzadikim, righteous ones, upon each of whom the world depends, are Messiahs transmigrated and reborn, not coming once but ever and in many persons, capable of being taken into anyone's soul, through and across roots and lineages. Hayyim Vital was whispered to be such a messiah, and he failed (though was not expected) to redeem his people in his lifetime. The Hidden Sages, though never named, include the likes of Abulafia, "The Ashkenazi," Joseph Karo, Joel Newberger, R. Akiva, Moses and that same Joshua, faithful to Allah. Tradition itself tells us we must look across lineages and religions, to be undeceived by time, in order to recognize coincidences such as Joseph's double-existence as single or continuous events that grasp us as with a purpose. Such events indicate not only the presence of the Mystery of our lodge, but the health of the Mystery, and of the M.O.C.A. at large.

Wherever we find and enjoy Moorish aesthetic we find Joseph Karo waiting in the ruins of the Temple for it to be raised again.

The prophet Noble Drew Ali was very likely familiar with the Hudson Valleyist Washington Irving's Alhambra, perhaps through a library, or overheard in Newark.

From Washington Irving, to Frederick Church's Olana, the Hudson River Painter's more-or-less-Moorish mansion (readily visible from the Catskill side of the Hudson River). From Noble Drew Ali to P. Lamborn-Wilson Bey (to put the two strands as briefly as possible).

The Moorish aesthetic is lavishly symbolical and cosmological, without requiring any particular referent. Lavish perhaps to the point of untrustworthiness, holy deceit. Here even lies, and the weirdest synthesis can and should join in celebration.

There is an undeniable fitness for the lodge of the M.O.C.A in Catskill N.Y.

ARCHITECTURES

1.

Thin cold sidles along the deer, their train, follows them like an angle laid at the foot of a living house, cold fact of means before it has taught us the heat of entry, the self it stands before, straddles, feeds.

Architecture of these loose bones worn passing near to one another, of cognizance turning into propinquity.

Open this stone. This bone. Cold season where another season leaps. Beneath the cold, soft inner back she presses against the marble column, the cold that surrounds us with columns, libraries, porticoes.

2.

I repeat myself, try to find passage from between, the closure of the circle *time* is. Escape from Albany!

I repeat to myself
the line's funny turn of the other on its way to self, kiss the face on the masthead.

3.

An angel comes from another town on some other errand.

We are known by our accidents: the fish your father caught with someone passing near,

angles of the house night yearns to turn, and turns into night.

4.

Night is a variety of wind, whistling across the corner of the house, to speak in a disturbance like human speech.

The lies I love,

angles yoke me to their machine, populate me with images, trains of thought, worms caught like fish from an unending motion.

5.

Both an individual and his worms glide through a cavernous gothic economy of grace, a being pocked with caves that are the lapses of ipseity, in which others live and glide past curves and down stairs, into the daring remainder of the body that's shared: and in the surprise of my motions other motives are exposed. We are being led somewhere. In the caves of Persia Zoroaster celebrated the cosmos, the descent of souls and their going out again from the body of Mithras. Focused graces in the caves of my days.

THE FOREST

1.

Amid the voices trees have heard and retained in the rings of their growth the mind cleans itself in their constant rain.

Speech is centerless, uninterrupted: say it once and say it forever, while each utterance is another person, a re-enactor. These are the clairvoyant who make war, who travel, and call out the ancient names of friends.

Who say everything, and stop, and start again.

The study of repetition. The insane at work.

2.

These are thoughts, allegiances—

3.

Aboard a forest the lone feather keeps up morale. Seamarks and portents, directionless signs of a consciousness also without direction. The drift of the *Wode* within the wood. Madness. Courtesie.

4.

The Wode totter, overrun by voices, free from sequence, eating berries. Flesh that does not decay, worlds within words.

The forest is crossed by lost cities, legions.

5.

The word for snake looks like any other word.

Snakes writhe from a nest of words, speaking of the Worm they will meet, and its quest that calls itself the past.

What words are attracted today as the Worm moves, calling rooms, windows, pathways. These are the individual snakes of the movement of the mind, the colors and memories, sleek propaganda for the slow sidewindering of days.

The worm forms a lineage the way a word seeks to be said.

I see the night of your heart's domain, and I see the snake that eats your heart.

I see the great serpent, the Schlong, and I feed myself to it.

Prose for St. Crispin & Crispinian's Day
(and also for Gerrit Lansing)

The Arms of the cross are Geminis in the wrong house, thighs sore.
In the painting by Bossche two executioners dance a turn around
the tree, and stab their knives into Crispin and Crispinian. As blood
flows to the foot of the cross, the spirit of Pharaoh speaks:

At the foot of the cross soak the bones of Adam, and the arms and
arms of the tree gather Calvarys and further examples to return for
love's pleasure. In number VI, the Lovers instruct a youth not in the
ways of love but how to cast and reel in. Love is gathered into Love.

Crispin and Crispinian were amazed, and the two Romans paddled
in silence. *Arma armisque cano,* hummed Pharaoh as he fingered
the loop atop the cross, and Crispin and Crispinian wondered at his
serial Misfortunes, and the City he was building.

GHOULS

Leaf damp underfoot the pace the peace of Fall scent and ascent I
padded quietly through graveyard gravings and decent wide passages
pal Thomas Cole and saw the last few natives slip through saw
pirates pulled spiritually if not literally from Salvator Rosa his
beauty and danger and the wilderness of human planning the
wilderness that appeals I saw at the Met among the continental
laborers finally someone to love Rosa a cocky Italian Faustus the
pirate peering into harbor unseen from a forested neck of land the
trees in their first blush of orange and gold red the final act of the
subject as it planned its ascent into the world awaiting breath plan
of painted and painter tied in their assault on the profane the heavy
Dutch vessel hidden now beneath Catskill cemetery sleepy bodies
stretching on white sand while Italian Native American ghouls
peer hidden from a neck of the mind ready to jump on uncounted,
unallowed, unhallowed, imperious *un-:* resplendent.

An Advertisement for Fanny Howe's *Night Philosophy* (Divided Publishing Ltd: 2020)

My child is 'talking' by the pellucid river of Gan Eden the pleasure garden as only childhood could be so sure of not knowing it and so knowing it in the arms of wisdom washerwoman Shekinah a child borne in the belly of the wind the secret of a secret like the wind in the trees tonight that cannot be touched but soothes take me into your keeping let me wake in your sleep the garden of God as Sarah suggests is the garden of pleasure rabbi's call this her secret saying as if the play of thought were the presence of coinherence she says in her secret waxed old shall I have pleasure . my lord being old also?

POET LAUREATE'S ADDRESS FOR THE OPENING OF CATSKILL'S BRIDGE TO HEAVEN

The poet wields authority in the assertions of poetry, not by the assertion of personal authority. In this the poet is a tribal chieftain, for whom any attempted exercise of authority would only be met with failure— failure of the poem— and the poet as chieftain would be ignored, and even punished. Language is of the people, and when the poet fails a poem by the undue usurpation of the means of language, this is tantamount not only to a failure of the poem but of the people.

The poet's only legitimate authority comes from surrender to the poem and to the language of its communication.

The Poet Laureate is a poet whose authority has been reiterated by a governing body. The authority of the P.L. is thus a civil authority, and the assertions of the P.L. are thus civic assertions: blessings, openings, closures, condemnations and curses.

The poet's surrender is the bridge between Heaven and Earth, and thus the Poet Laureate makes civic matters both Heavenly and Earthly: is pontifex (pons + facere), bridge maker, priest.

Consider the Uncle Sam bridge, and the recent restoration of the so-called Black Bridge: now all that remains to restore the village of Catskill (or, *Tripontium!*) to its former three-bridge dignity is the reopening of the "through truss bridge."

By the triple authority of the Laureateship, I declare the so-called "through truss bridge" built by the Catskill Mountain Railway in 1881, and removed in 1918, to be a bridge from Earth to Heaven and vice versa, and open to the commerce of the public.

***

(A slightly altered version of this Bridge Opening was used to open the Brooklyn Bridge, at Berl's Poetry Shop on March 5th, 2020. In that version the last two paragraphs appear thus:

The Brooklyn Bridge, designed by Washington Roebling, is that hybrid cable-stayed/suspension bridge which spans the East River between the boroughs of Manhattan and Brooklyn; built with then famous Rosendale cement, and crushed blue-stone from the Catskill Mountains. Much of this material would have passed through the then Laureateless Village of Catskill, now under my jurisdiction, by train or from it's busy docks city bound.

By the triple authority of the Laureateship, I declare the so-called "Brooklyn Bridge" opened May 24th 1883, to be a bridge from Earth to Heaven and vice versa, and open to the commerce of the public.)

A CELEBRATION OF VILLAGE LAWS AS THE BUREAUCRACY OF THE HEAVENLY CITY

Speech Delivered by the Village of Catskill Poet Laureate (disgraced)

A quarter of the way down the hill of Division Street running perpendicularly west is a gravel path, seven or so feet in width and approx. 96 paces in length, that serves to connect Division Street to the terminus of Thompson street, where that meets the dugout of Catskill High School's baseball field.

This unnamed lane was first brought to my attention by fellow townspeople whose property adjoins it, who informed me that though running through their property, this lane is in fact by local law & custom a public lane open to all who wish to lead their livestock into the heart of our town, with its docks and warehouses, butcheries and auctions.

Here the law survives in a portion of what must have been a more extensive Cattle Road, used by such drovers as would have stayed in the drover's hotel, and drunk at the Bull's Head tavern in town— the Bull's Head whose sign, now vanished, was painted by local artist and poet Thomas Cole.

This law survives along with innumerable other laws and unclaimed privileges in scraps of land forgotten among us.

Property is the spell of capital, and the law is its enforcement. But there can be no capital without property in the same way that there is no law without the practice of the law. Thus the law is at bottom ceremony, and when the purpose of the law is removed from the needs of Capital, the Poet Laureate is its conductor.

With the generous gift of ten bulls by Story Farm of Catskill; by the donation of textiles by Les Indiennes of Hudson and by the fashioning of these into ceremonial horn-coverings, flags and capes to adorn the livestock by the excellent Ladies of the St. Luke's Episcopal Church of Catskill Cooking Club, we may observe a rare and unusual aspect of law's function: the ceremonial resurrection of a contract which is visible and only ever extant in its symbolic fragments.

The rite that ties the lion's head to the man's body, and the animal's body to the walls of one's mind, and one person to another. Law that does not tend toward absolute ownership, but is itself the celebratory symbol of living bonds beyond either reason or control, thus not a dead-end, but a liberation.

IV. Associations

STARTS

Arithmetic. Saffron.
What money meant to be:
memory. I'm going to blow it all.
Live off charity
the fruit that hangs over the sidewalk
and cannot deceive us.

Elements. Arguments.
The troublesome oneness
we suffer to take possession
speaks from the graveyard
not speaks but thinks
trusty barley in the hand.

Candor. Anchor.
The place meant.
Eden I'm remembering
turn the table lengthwise
for feng shui, matter deceives
fallen from its placement.
Secret calculus. Put it back.

The Alone. The Aloe.
Cutlasses laid across your path.
The broad of the sword confers, warns;
we have already crawled across its
sharp test, to know, to coast
safe from happening, from selves
the glowing people we get to watch.

Eager. Ärger.
Mustn't doubt what appeals.
What fiery nature
forms, and then admits
to destruction as if there were
no forms besides desire:
the salamander thriving
in its flames. This
curve, excitement
in which I swim.

Deshalb. Cataramonachia.
therefore is only half the story:
a curse told over the eucharist.
Spoiled meat killed Sangjay,
black magic of all illness.
These devils we build with.

Mist. Armistice.
History before it reaches time.
We walk through the garden.

Caliper. Juniper.
Seizing upon the halves of things
sizzles in the mineral dank.
The flanks of bison, elk heads, herds
that are the halves of herds,
the boy and the girl shepherds seek their heavenly descent:
while the shaman who is only half
cries from the earth.
Mind is this pasture

with the animals we run among,
wary of shadow men, and their shadow animals,
their sheep that mix discreetly with ours
their language I pretend not to understand.

Sacred Harp. Quaker Meet.
the movement of the spirit across your me's
pray with our geometry
focus pocus, maneuvering the crystal
in which I hold myself.
No mirror is far from home.

Arduous. Ardor.
The lover quakes at the beloved's feet,
and if she's the castratrix Cybele
distance is a measure of mercy
the grace of being Appalachian
or some other ache,
that finds its way to speak
become closer than
be already you.

Salmoned. Soiled.
The mere fact of you
pretends to go by.

Bloom. Elbow.
Refulgence at the bend of things
suppleness and then sudden darknesses
as they turn away and glow in turning

pretending to obscure what
we used to call the subconscious mind
I mean this thin figure in flight across the field
spelling words I cannot read. Resist.

Frills. Affronts.
Thrill I was thinking of
cognition is recognition
catching them by surprise.

Rain. Array.
No silence can be like another
unless they have this music in common.

Fall. Resurrection.
First, the Purifier,
with which we clean the cup.
Then the Silent Butler,
that quiets our crumbs.

ASSOCIATIONS

fervent

Desire is easily burnt
the self and its opposite

rejections are boarders
nimble damp pirates
our ancestors left behind
to haunt some forsaken interior
like an extra strand of *dna*

opposition is other, eager.

servant

I withdraw my finger knowingly from the entries in this missing
book. Hand-signs are not abstractions. I ring the kitchen bell, set the
table, a cigarette out back of the merely physical with the servant
girls Botticelli once drew right in front of me. Here. One day I'll
show you.

salient, serpent

The damn angle that assaults me from the particles of my routine
in my role as an adjunct of the turquoise palace. I can hear them
hammer as I lie full length on the blue couch. Hands crossed
Egyptian-style clutch a brightly painted wooden easter-egg and a
fresh stalk of tansy. Their cigarette ash clatters like eagles against
the smooth green sky.

cirrus

Curl of hair that is pleased. Finger,

how do we please our fingers,
so they curl up and show
go this way, or go away

as in the story of God's hands
we don't work for you no more

as if He (the She of the story)
were a quality of abandonment,
the shadows gathered by unruly rhymes.

An advertisement for Kevin Opstedal's *Pacific Standard Time* (UDP:2019)

perfected beneath a long flowing gown

The erratic gold we were used to.
Turned out it was all surplus,

windfall of the nuevo rich
as with any -ism we gloried in shame,
and were burned into shape

by gold I mean cowries, chunks of tarmac,
someone's grandparents at Goodwill

burning logs around a blue lake,
in so-called Afghanistan

Colgate or North-South Lake most likely.
What we know is where we are, huddled in
a flower like other things too bright to be seen.

personal blood ties & the visions elicited by them

At your indiscretion,
as portrayed by regal Weeping Spruce

I lug my ignorance to Jakob Böhme
the wheels of my surfboard useless
        in the stringy red tide
until I can't remember the plot of *Signatura Rerum*
only the name Böhrmen in my hands, the tide going out
with its extra terminal 'n'
as Coleridge would have said it,
and Duncan's majestic merman 'r' avid within.

I wrap my mouth around this familiar old shoe
like a stationary-bike ride
extra-wide cigarettes soaked in lamb's blood
        tucked into my dog-skin cap
winter morning across the Atlantean graveyard
I insist until you don't believe me is not resting under Europe.

the shadows in this town are all wrong

Another town's shadows turn here
before rest, tail under chin

where do we learn these postures from
I asked like some facetious Yankee
as if to turn my homage into a pastiche

pardon my reach

these somersaults are for the Virgin Mary

I don't mind if you duck for cover in the pews

in Santa Cruz or Guangzhou
not that that's where you live.

Still, it's cheapest to let the imps convert our currency,
their meagerly subversive knives flashing
                                below the bridge
where unadulterated rhymes crash
        like a coal-powered mouth-harp
        through my persona's wooden teeth.

BRETON INTERLINEAR

Toujours pour la premiére fois

Horses, lizards, cars in the snow
snap decisions
with the cry of crows in the neighborhood.

Maison tout imaginaire

Ask the loaded birds
not the pallid prism from which they hurl
jet-streams and islands: their
enduring flashes through the imagination.
Heat lightning. Snow lightning. Fire in the water.

La déchirure unique

I am certain that I'm reading your mind
Across the chasm mind opens. Telepathy
flows from home, an energetic rift.

Oú tu m'apparais seule.

EVEN STEVENS

1.
The meadow has a wild backwards shadow.
In the white gloom in spring the ice resumes
its forward motion through the air and packs
its listless ways into the disc of summer.
At the Tivoli Bays the rain falls up and down.
Amid the tides and currents there is nothing
to salvage in this house, only the alarm recurrent
and hidden shudders in its illusion of walls.

2.
By the spicy smoking fountain it is a pleasure to watch
position and opposition knowing them to be imposture.
Even water is improved by the hiding of it, and where
the timeless idlers hide themselves they contract
apparent activity, flavors. Their smooth gems in my path again.

3.
An homage is not less original or lacking
the unoriginal lack that haunts our vale
with lacustrine slanted light, through nights
infested with acanthus and jasmine like switches
on a wall that are hidden by an open door.
This lake is carried on the tendrils of its light, shoots
demotic extensions of the unreal. Detached fingers
wake beyond the extensions of charmed sleep.

To quote your ghost, Estabon, Garland of Flowers:
"The unreal comes directly at us, the real
does not assess." And:
"When thought is backwards, resilience is real."

THE FOUNTAINEER

A string of birds
upon a breeze I rummage
on the pool's surface.

What you overhear
you oversee.

Whoever I am
sitting on your knee
your finger wedged
within my spine
that column of hollow
subjunctives,
the sea.

Read my lips,
minds, thighs,
leaves
reading reading
we osculate
reply reply
glorious, made up.

I used to hang out
at the fountain of youth.
A super-physical language
I learned as I swam;
and delight's adjudications
danced within my matter.

The fountains that lurk throughout these woods with retrospective
need hunt us down like vampires with the other singing animals. The
self is an enchantment. Under the wings of parrots long extinct from

these shores, goblins fan the cheap human flames we carry in hand mirrors around their mountain kingdom; their kingdom, now and then, briefly demolished by errant children.

ACKNOWLEDGMENTS

BOOKS I & II:

Some of these poems have appeared in *Caesura Mag* (Austin Carder); *Columba Poetry* (Emily Tristan Jones); *Blazing Stadium*; *Green Kill Broadsheet* (Tom Romeo); *The Wax Paper* (Chloe Bliss Snyder).

BOOK III:

"The Face: a tribute to Achorai" was written in response to a collaborative work by Robert Kelly and Joel Newberger, called Achorai. Achorai is the Hebrew term used to denote the "hinder parts of God" when they were shown to Moses.

"Manifesto: on the Aesthetics of Solomon's Temple" first appeared in *The Doris.*

"For the Moorish Israelites of Catskill" first appeared in *The Moorish Science Monitor: Inaugural for the South Pointing Lodge of Catskill, NY.*

"Architectures" first appeared in *Aurochs II* (Stephen Williams).

"Poet Laureate's Address for the Opening of Catskill's Bridge to Heaven" appeared as a Village Bulletin broadsheet, published by the *Offices of the Poet Laureate/Arts Ambassador 2020.* (Shortly after publishing the initial bridge opening ceremony, for reasons unimportant here, I formally abdicated my position as Poet Laureate, though I have not and will not renounce the authority that accompanies that position.)

"A Celebration of Village Laws as the Bureaucracy of the Heavenly City" appeared in *Blazing Stadium* Issue 4.

BOOK IV:

The poems titled "Starts," "Associations," and "for Kevin Opstedal," were published as *Associations* by *The Swan* (University of Pennsylvania). Many thanks to Joel Newberger.

The poems "Even Stevens" and "The Fountaineer" appeared in a video aired in the poetry section curated by CA Conrad for the twitch tv channel Transmissions2020.

Further Thanks:
Billie Chernicoff, Lila Dunlap, Whit Griffin, Alex Hampshire, Ann Lauterbach, Vlad Nahitchevansky, George Quasha, Charles Stein, Robert Tomlinson, Peter Lamborn Wilson

Cover image: engraving from the title page of Elias Ashmole's *Theatrum Chemicum Britannicum,* 1652; from Adam McLean's Gallery of alchemical images.

ABOUT THE AUTHOR

Tamas Panitz was born in Budapest, Hungary, in 1992, and is a Gemini of Romany heritage. He spent some wretched years growing up in Maryland, and some excellent years elsewhere. He graduated Bard College in 2014, and lives in the Catskills.

Panitz is a founding editor of the online journal *Blazing Stadium.* He was the Village of Catskill, New York, Poet Laureate—a post from which he resigned. His poetry has been translated into Spanish, and is currently being translated into Georgian. Panitz owns dictionaries in Hungarian, French, Spanish, Italian, German, Haitian Creole, Chinese, Ancient Egyptian, Mayan, Modern and Ancient Greek, Latin, and Hebrew, and can speak some of those languages quite poorly.

He is the author of several books of poetry, most recently: *The House of the Devil* (Lunar Chandelier Collective: 2020).

Panitz is also a painter, whose paintings and stray poems can be found on instagram, @tamaspanitz.

www.ingramcontent.com/pod-product-compliance
Lightning Source LLC
Chambersburg PA
CBHW031006090426
42737CB00008B/699